Drama Play

Also available:

The Teddy Bears' Picnic and Other Stories: Role Play in the Early Years: Drama Activities for 3- to 7-year-olds by Jo Boulton and Judith Ackroyd (1 84312 123 9)

Pirates and Other Adventures: Role Play in the Early Years: Drama Activities for 3- to 7-year-olds by Jo Boulton and Judith Ackroyd (1 84312 124 7)

The Toymaker's Workshop and Other Tales: Role Play in the Early Years: Drama Activities for 3- to 7-year-olds by Jo Boulton and Judith Ackroyd (1 84312 125 5)

Drama Play

Bringing Books to Life through Drama for 4–7 year-olds

Kay Hiatt

David Fulton Publishers

This edition reprinted 2007 by Routledge
2 Park Square, Milton Park, Abingdon, Oxon, OX14 4RN
Simultaneously published in the USA and Canada
By Routledge
270 Madison Avenue, New York, NY 10016

First published in Great Britain in 2006 by David Fulton Publishers

10 9 8 7 6 5 4 3 2

Note: The right of Kay Hiatt to be identified as the author of this work has been asserted by her in accordance with the Copyright, Designs and Patents Act 1988.

British Library Cataloguing in Publication Data
A catalogue record for this book is available from the British Library.

ISBN: 1 84312 178 6

Typeset by FiSH Books, London
Printed and bound in Great Britain

Contents

Acknowlegements

I am grateful to the following organisations for allowing the use of their copyright material to be reproduced in this book:

HIT Entertainment plc, for the use of the Bob the Builder image (p. 21 and Plate 3.1)

Frances Lincoln Ltd, for the following (see plate section):

Tabby Cat's Secret by Kathy Henderson, illustrated by Susan Winter. Copyright © 2002

Next! by Christopher Inns. Copyright © 2001

The Gift of the Sun by Dianne Stewart, illustrated by Jude Daly. Copyright © 1996

The Leopard's Drum – text, illustrations and design by Jessica Souhami and Paul McAlinden. Copyright © 1995

Camille and the Sunflowers by Laurence Anholt. Copyright © 1994

Rama and the Demon King – text, illustratins and design by Jessica Souhami and Paul McAlinden. Copyright © 1997

Introduction

Drama play: bringing books to life through drama

Drama is an important teaching tool which engages pupils and stimulates their thinking skills and their imagination. The aim of this book is to offer very practical guidance for a range of drama techniques which can be used to 'bring books to life' so that children can engage intellectually and emotionally with their contents.

The benefits of drama

- Children will be willing to 'play' alongside you.
- They will be engaged, interested and having fun.
- Their thinking and problem-solving skills will improve.
- Their emotional intelligence will be developed through identifying and responding to another character's situation.
- Their speaking and listening skills will be shaped up and honed through frequent use of just a few drama techniques.
- Their written outcomes will be far better than might have been expected.
- Their reading will be 'comprehended' at a much higher level than might have been expected.

There are important links with drama in several other initiatives which are currently underway in primary schools.

1. Drama and *Excellence and Enjoyment*

Excellence and Enjoyment: A Strategy for Primary Schools was published by the DfES in 2003. It describes the best practice of outstanding primary schools where 'children are engaged by learning that develops and stretches them and excites their imagination – not just learning different things, but learning in many different ways – they offer rich, exciting programmes of learning'. Drama is very well placed as a learning tool to develop, stretch and excite children's imaginations.

2. Drama and 'Speaking and Listening'

The Primary National Strategy also published in 2003 *Speaking, Listening, Learning: Working with Children in Key Stages 1 and 2*, because 'speaking and listening lie at the heart of almost all effective learning', and the materials give drama an equal place alongside speaking, listening, group discussion and interaction.

Most drama objectives from these materials are supported by *Drama Play*. These are:

Drama Year 1 – Term 1, Term 2, Term 3

4. to explore familiar themes and characters through improvisation and role-play

8. to act out own and well-known stories, using different voices for characters

12. to discuss why they like a performance

Drama Year 2 – Term 1, Term 2, Term 3

16. to adopt appropriate roles in small or large groups and consider alternative courses of action

20. to consider how mood and atmosphere are created in a live or recorded performance

24. to present parts of traditional stories, own stories or work from different parts of the curriculum for members of their class

3. Drama and Accelerated Learning

Alasdair Smith's book, *Accelerated Learning in the Classroom*, which has had significant influence in primary schools, advocates 'Effective, balanced, whole-brain learning is rich, multi-path, multi-sensory learning'. Drama provides for all of these as it crosses all types of learning – visual, auditory and kinaesthetic. In addition, drama is easily accessible for all pupils, whatever their backgrounds or starting points.

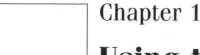

Chapter 1

Using this book

The aim of this book is to help teachers use a range of simple drama techniques with confidence and enjoyment. These are outlined in Chapter 2. A series of ready-planned lesson ideas are then offered based on 12 high-quality books for four- to seven-year-olds. All these books are currently in print and easily available from bookshops; several of them are likely to have been purchased already by schools and some are available in Big Book format.

Drama techniques used in the lessons are signalled by the use of different symbols, so that teachers have a quick reference guide for what they will be doing. Every lesson clearly describes what other resources will be needed.

After using the ideas outlined in *Drama Play*, teachers should be confident in applying them to any good-quality book. In addition, the drama techniques are extremely useful to use across the curriculum with particularly strong links to history, geography, religious education, PSHE, science and art.

To support a whole-school approach to drama, there are two monitoring sheets provided in Appendix 1. These are to be used by teachers, co-ordinators and head teachers. In addition, a list of 15 tried and tested books is provided as Appendix 2.

The 12 titles used in *Drama Play* are listed below, followed by a brief summary of the story.

4–5-year-olds

***Bob's Birthday* by Emma Fogden, published by BBC (ISBN: 0 563 47653 2)**

Bob is disappointed when everyone seems to have forgotten his birthday. However, everything turns out well as Wendy has arranged a surprise birthday party for Bob and his friends.

Tabby Cat's Secret **by Kathy Henderson, published by Frances Lincoln (ISBN: 0 7112 1882 X)**

While the house is being decorated, Tabby Cat leaves and finds a surprising place to have her kittens.

Next! **by Christopher Inns, published by Frances Lincoln (ISBN: 0 7112 1696 7)**

Set in a toy hospital, Doctor Hopper and Nurse Rex Barker help the sick toys get better.

Snail Trail **by Ruth Brown, published by Anderson Press (ISBN: 0 86264 949 8)**

Slimy Snail sets out on his trail through the garden and finally goes to sleep.

5–6-year-olds

The Gift of the Sun **by Dianne Stewart, published by Frances Lincoln (ISBN: 0 7112 1021 7)**

Thulani is lazy and sells off all his animals – in spite of this, he and his wife become rich!

*Anancy and Mr Dry-Bone **by Fiona French, published by Frances Lincoln (ISBN: 0 7112 0787 9)**

Two suitors, one rich, the other poor, attempt to win the hand of Miss Louise. Rich Mr Dry-bone fails whereas poor but clever Anancy succeeds.

Home Before Dark **by Ian Beck, published by Hippo (ISBN: 0 590 19918 8)**

Teddy is dropped by Lily in the park on a cold and windy evening. After several adventures he manages to get home.

***The Leopard's Drum* by Jessica Souhami, published by Frances Lincoln (ISBN: 0 7112 0907 3)**

Osebo the leopard has a magnificent drum and Nyame the Sky God wants it. Several animals try to get it for him but only one is clever enough to succeed – Achi-cheri, the tortoise.

6–7-year-olds

****Camille and the Sunflowers* by Laurence Anholt, published by Frances Lincoln (ISBN: 0 7112 1050 0)**

This book offers a glimpse of Van Gogh's life through the eyes of a young boy, Camille. It also helps to develop an awareness of the importance of friendship which can combat, but not always overcome, local prejudice towards a stranger in town.

****Rama and the Demon King* by Jessica Souhami, published by Frances Lincoln (0 7112 1158 2)**

This is the story of the brave and good prince Rama and his battle against Ravana, the evil ten-headed king of all demons.

****Little Inchkin* by Fiona French, published by Frances Lincoln (ISBN: 0 7112 0917 0)**

This is a charming story of a Japanese 'Tom Thumb', whose determination to prove himself results in a glittering prize – normal stature and the hand of a beautiful princess.

****The Fire Children* by Eric Maddern, published by Frances Lincoln (ISBN: 0 7112 0885 9)**

Two spirit people land on Earth and make their home in a cave. They make some clay children to keep them company but Nyame, the Sky-God, keeps making unexpected visits – with some surprising results.

---

* Also available as a Big Book

An outline of useful drama techniques

Freeze-frame

Children select a key moment from a story and create a still picture to illustrate what is happening. When the teacher calls freeze, pupils remain still, holding the action for a moment in time.

Using the list of key events provided for each book the class can create a series of pictures to represent the whole story from beginning to end – this is an excellent way to prepare children for writing complete stories.

Improvisation

Children improvise the conversation in the freeze-frame with no prior planning, in role as characters from the story.

Thought tracking

The private thoughts or reactions of a character are spoken publicly. Characters in a freeze-frame can be tapped on the shoulder by a teacher or a child – this signals that the child in role must speak his/her thoughts aloud. This technique is very useful for developing inference and deduction skills and story theme.

Decision alley

A central character facing a dilemma in the drama moves slowly between two lines of children formed by the rest of the group. As s/he passes each person, those on one side comment aloud in support of a course of action, while those on the other side give reasons against it. At the end of the alley, the character has to make a decision based on what s/he has heard.

Diaries, letters, messages

Written in or out of role as if by characters who are part of the story. These pieces of writing may affect the drama in some way, e.g. change the course of action. A letter may request that the children do something, e.g. write replies to the character who wrote it, offering advice etc.

Dynamic duos

Improvisational conversations in pairs, each child acting as a character linked to the plot. The conversations are a retelling of what has happened so far in the story, and their personal views on this. The teacher allows a few of the conversations to be 'overheard' by the rest of the class so that children can experience and reflect on the views of others.

Props

Items which appear in a story or which are used to trigger a new story, e.g. items found and brought into the classroom.

Toys and puppets

Used as main characters from the story who can talk about what has happened. They can also be used as a stimulus for writing new stories.

Mantle of the expert

In the role of specialists, e.g. scientists, farmers, the children present what they have learned about a topic. Most beneficial when linked to the technique of 'jigsawing' as outlined in the DfES materials on speaking and listening.

Maps/diagrams

Drawing small maps or diagrams provides a concrete reference for the events which take place in a story.

Meetings

Involving the whole group in the same place at the same time within a dramatic context linked to the story.

Teacher in role

Teacher acts the part of a character in a scene or a situation. S/he can challenge the children to develop their ideas further in the dramatic situation.

Children in role

Children act the parts of characters in a scene or situation.

Hot seating

One child or more can be in role. The rest of the class should be forewarned and prepare questions to ask the child/children in role.

A vital speaking and listening classroom strategy

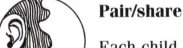

Pair/share

Each child has a partner with whom they can discuss possible answers to 'open-ended' questions posed by the teacher. They can also prepare questions to ask the 'teacher in role' or children in role (hot seating). Activities should be limited to a maximum of two minutes.

Chapter 2

Key drama techniques exemplified through 'Red Riding Hood'

'Red Riding Hood' is a useful story through which to demonstrate drama techniques as part of your teaching repertoire.

The story

Red Riding Hood is told by her mother to go and visit her grandmother who lives in another part of the wood. Her mother packs a basket with bread, butter, jam, cake and some medicine and gives this to Red Riding Hood. Before she leaves, her mother warns her not to leave the path, but to go directly to her grandmother's cottage.

Red Riding Hood leaves home and begins her journey. However on the way she decides to leave the path to pick some flowers. While she is doing this she is spotted by a wolf, who decides to find out where she is going.

Although surprised by the wolf, she explains what she is doing and tells him where she is going. He suggests that she should collect some more flowers and he runs off to Grandmother's cottage.

He knocks on the door, pretending to be Red Riding Hood, and Grandma opens it. She is swallowed whole and he dresses up in some of her clothes, gets into bed and pretends to be her.

Red Riding Hood enters the cottage, is a little suspicious, then realises 'Grandmother' is the wolf and is saved just in time by the woodcutter who hears her screams. The wolf is killed with one swipe of his axe and Grandma emerges from the wolf's tummy – shaken but safe! (see plate section, illustration no. 2.1.)

Key events

Red Riding Hood and Mother in the cottage.

Packing the basket.

Mother telling her not to leave the path.

Red Riding Hood skipping along.

Red Riding Hood leaving the path and picking the flowers.

Talking to the wolf.

The wolf knocking on the cottage door.

The wolf swallowing Grandma in one go.

The wolf dressing up in Grandma's clothes.

Red Riding Hood talking to the wolf.

The woodcutter raising his axe.

A chart like the one above is very useful for children to be able to review the key events as a basis for freeze-frames, improvisations, retelling the story and writing the story in their own words. It is also useful for planning a similar story but with different characters. Boys in general find it more difficult than girls to remember the complete sequence of events in a story. The events above can be the basis of the freeze-frames.

Preparing the freeze-frames

With help, children select the key moments from Red Riding Hood and create a series of still pictures to illustrate what is happening. The teacher may guide them in creating the freeze-frames, aiming to get as many children as possible to take part. Key characters are played by different children in each frame.

Some children may need more help from the teacher, e.g. talking them through what to show, helping them to position themselves; more experienced children will discuss and plan this independently.

The teacher 'photographs' each frame, using the words *'Starting positions – freeze!'* The frame is frozen for a few seconds, and then s/he moves on to the next frame, the 'click' of the camera signalling the end of one scene and the start of another. The whole story can be moved through quite quickly, frame by frame.

A digital camera can also be used to record and print off the whole sequence of freeze-frames, which can be used as a source for discussion, reflection, mapping the story, writing captions or retelling the story.

Boys in particular find this concrete illustration of the story very useful for supporting their short-term memory and interest in order to retell a story.

Improvisation

Children make up or improvise dialogue with one or more characters, or their 'spoken thoughts' if there is only one character in the scene. It is linked to freeze-frames, thought tracking and retelling in role for dynamic duos.

Improvisation linked to freeze-frames

After each freeze-frame has been watched by the class, the teacher asks each group to improvise a conversation, or to think aloud through using the 'thought tracking' device, as described below. Different children can take part this time while the rest of the class watches. In 'Red Riding Hood' the children can improvise the conversation Red Riding Hood had with her mother before leaving the cottage and on meeting the wolf etc.

This happens in the following sequence:

- 'Starting positions – freeze!'
- 'Action' (improvisation)
- 'Click' – of the camera signalling the end of the scene

The teacher can encourage children watching to offer constructive comments on the way the scene was acted.

Thought tracking

This device is used when a character is alone, or when a character turns to the audience, facing away from the other character(s), and speaks aloud what s/he is *really* thinking. These thoughts are based on the character's current situation.

The child is tapped on the shoulder by another child or teacher. This signals the start of the improvised speech.

In 'Red Riding Hood', she could be asked about how she feels, or what is she thinking about, at key moments in the drama, e.g. leaving the cottage, walking through the woods, meeting the wolf.

Decision alley

Every story has its decision moment when the story develops further, thus sustaining the interest of the reader. Red Riding Hood's development point happens when she decides to leave the path, in spite of her mother's warning not to do so.

This is an interesting area to explore with children, and it helps them to consider cause and effect of characters' decisions. It can also be used across the curriculum, including Personal Health and Social Education (PSHE) and citizenship, as a creative way of thinking about and resolving problem situations, e.g. pushing each other in a queue, or name calling of any kind.

In Red Riding Hood, half the class stands on one side of her and half on the other side.

The left-hand side has to think of reasons why she should not leave the path, e.g. it could be dangerous, you might see a wolf, you might get lost, you might fall over, you might fall into a river. The right-hand side tells her why she should go off the path, e.g. there could be some flowers, blackberries, birds, or butterflies, or a short cut to Granny's house.

When she reaches the end of the alley she must turn and speak aloud her thoughts and then make a decision on a course of action.

Letters, messages

These may be placed to fall out of the back of the book as you are reading it, or be 'delivered' to your school, e.g. a week after this book has been finished, a letter may arrive, signed by Big Bad Wolf, saying he wants some advice from the class on how to make more friends.

Writing in role

Writing in role is a powerful way to engage children's imaginations and there are a number of opportunities to do this in Red Riding Hood, e.g.

● A letter to Red Riding Hood from her father, advising her not to go off the path again, giving at least two reasons why it may be unwise

● A letter of apology from the wolf to Grandmother, saying that he will never frighten her again

● A recipe for biscuits to send to Granny from Red Riding Hood's mother

● A warning notice written by the woodcutter, saying what might happen if children do not stay on the path

● A labelled map of the story setting

● A series of pictures telling the story (storyboarding). The pictures can be labelled.

Dynamic duos

The class is instructed to get into pairs, each of which is given the same role – one is Red Riding Hood, the other is her best friend whom she meets in the woods. Red Riding Hood recounts to her friend the story of the day she visited Grandmother.

While they are doing this the teacher moves around the whole class, listening to the conversations. The teacher can ask a few of the duos, one pair at a time, to carry on their conversation while the rest of the class listens.

Props

It is a powerful experience for the class if the teacher brings in something real, e.g. honey, bread, apples, medicine and spoon, which can be used by the children as they pack a basket for Grandmother.

Teacher in role

The teacher should tell the class what will happen. It is not necessary to have any props or dressing-up clothes as children at this young age just believe who you are. However, the teacher can have a prop if s/he wants to, e.g. a basket to hold showing she is Red Riding Hood or a mob cap to wear as Grandma.

Going into role

A simple strategy is for the teacher to stand up, saying that when s/he has turned around and sat down, s/he will be a different person, e.g. Red Riding Hood. Once in role the teacher can say 'Hello, thank you for inviting me to your class', or, to remind them who she is, 'Hello, my name is Red Riding Hood.'

If they have thought about or written any questions, a prompt could be 'Would you like to ask me anything about what happened to me the day I went to Grandmother's cottage?' To remind them about where Red Riding Hood has come from, she could say 'It was raining in the forest today but the birds were singing...' If they are slow to ask anything, a question, e.g. 'Have you ever been on a walk through a forest?' will start them off.

Coming out of role

It is important for the teacher to tell the children, several times, that s/he is now out of role; some children may become quite anxious if they think s/he is still in role as someone else.

Several children/class in role

The teacher can ask a group of children or the whole class to go into group role e.g. half the class as Red Riding Hood, half the class as Grandmother. It is best for them to be given a few minutes to prepare questions they would like to ask; Y2 pupils could write questions down on their whiteboards. The teacher can direct questions at each half of the class, or different members of the group can ask questions of the other character. This is interesting because different children can pose questions in role.

Hot seating

One or more children go into role as a character or characters, sitting in front of the class. They must prepare for this by having a discussion beforehand about what they know about that character. This will ensure that they can give quality responses to the questions from the class. It is useful if a teaching assistant can help them rehearse this.

The class should also prepare questions to ask the children who are in role. In 'Red Riding Hood', these could be Grandmother, the woodcutter, the wolf, Red Riding Hood, her mother. One, several or all of the characters can be 'hot seated 'together.

Mantle of the expert

This is a very useful device whereby children are in role as an 'expert' of some kind. They prepare a short presentation to the class linked to any aspect of the curriculum. The 'jigsaw' approach to group information gathering and sharing would fit well with the 'mantle of the expert 'approach.

The expert in 'Red Riding Hood' could be the woodcutter talking about the life of the forest or Red Riding Hood's mother talking about how to look after elderly people.

Maps/diagrams

The teacher or children could draw a map of the setting and the route characters take in the story.

In 'Red Riding Hood', this could represent her walk to the cottage, showing the path she walked along to pick the flowers.

Chapter 3

Foundation Stage Reception class (4–5-year-olds)

Links to early learning goals

Bob's Birthday – 'People Who Help Us'

Builders/painters/decorators. A role-play area could be set up with the help of the children either inside or outside the setting, e.g. a workshop, a DIY superstore, a building site. The sand tray could be used as a mini-building site with the help of Bob the Builder toys. Adults who work in the building trade could be invited in to talk about what they do.

ICT link

Use Google (images) and search for 'Bob the Builder'. Create a folder of photographs with the help of the children and encourage them to view these on screen and talk about them together.

Tabby Cat's Secret – 'Our Pets'

Vet/nurse. A role-play area, e.g. a vet's waiting room and surgery, could be set up with children helping by collecting a number of toys and deciding what is wrong with them. They could bandage a cat's paw or head, or write a label, e.g. the dog is ill; this rabbit will not eat. Parents could bring in pets and talk about them – some kittens would be a bonus!

ICT link

Use Google (images) and search for 'pets' in general or particular pets with the help of the children, e.g. kittens, hamsters, puppies. Create a folder of photographs with the help of the children and encourage them to view these on screen and talk about them together. Get them to paint different pets, draw several 'on screen' and place them alongside the photos.

Next! – 'Our Toys'

With the help of the children, a toy shop and a toy hospital could be set up as two interlinked areas. Grandparents could bring in some of their toys so that children could see older toys such as peg dolls and Meccano.

ICT link

Use Google (images) and search for 'toys' in general, then 'old toys' with the help of the children. Create a folder of photographs with the children's help and encourage them to view these on screen and talk about them together.

Snail Trail – 'Mini-Beasts'

With the help of an adult who can remind them of the sequence of events in the story, children could set up their own 'snail trail' in the sand pit, a space or the outdoor play area. Toy or clay snails could be used. The 'snail trail' search on Google below will give pictures of patterns created by artists, based on snails' trails, which could stimulate the children to create big floor patterns, indoors or outside.

ICT link

Use Google (images) and search for 'snails' then 'snail trail' with the help of the children. Create a folder of photographs with the help of the children and encourage them to view these on screen and talk about them together.

Bob's Birthday by Emma Fogden

Summary of the story

Bob is disappointed when everyone seems to have forgotten his birthday. However, everything is okay as Wendy has arranged a surprise birthday party (see plate section, illustration no. 3.1).

Key events

Wendy tells Bob's friends to pretend that they have all forgotten about his birthday.

He goes off to work feeling really unhappy.

As soon as he has gone Wendy starts making his birthday cake and wraps all his presents.

When Bob and all the workers return they are very pleased to see the party table and they all wish Bob a 'Happy Birthday'.

Resources

Stories about Bob the Builder, published by the BBC, e.g. *Bob's Birthday*, *The House that Bob Built*, *Roley and the Rock Star*, *Roley's Animal Rescue*; book and tape packs; videos; magazines – Bob the Builder magazines which have been cut up and placed into A4 plastic booklets available from most large newsagents; Big Books – a Big Book made from the children's paintings and drawings. The teacher can write out the captions which the children would like to add to the pictures.

Drama techniques

Role-play.

Early learning goals

The focus early learning goal for this activity is Communication, Language and Literacy (CLL), but a number of other goals can be supported through preparing for the party.

Teacher and children in role

- Show the cover of the book and then go into role as Bob. Tell the children that you are very unhappy today because it's your birthday and everyone has forgotten about it and no one has even wished you 'Happy Birthday'.

- Come out of role.

- Read the book up to the part where Bob goes off to work.

- Tell the children that they will be helping to make things for Bob's birthday.

- Have ready an empty table.

Ask the children what they should make for Bob's birthday party. Write a list on a big piece of paper and use it as the plan for activities for the rest of the week. Some of them may make cakes (play dough or real), others could wrap up presents which they will choose themselves, some can make birthday cards, and several can help to decorate a real or make-believe cake. Others can make paper hats, collect paper plates, make some jelly and so on.

Writing activity

- Have some examples of invitations for them to see and help them to compose some of their own for Bob's party.

- Make a big version of Bob's song (see *Bob the Builder: Bob's Birthday*, Penguin Character Books, ISBN 0 563 55655 2) and get the children to learn it and sing it.

Children in role

- Ask the children to lay the table.

- When Bob appears (you in role) children can all sing the song.

- Then the party can take place.

Children helping to set up their own role-play areas: a builder's yard

- Tell the class that you have had a text message on your mobile phone asking you to set up a builder's yard.

- Read them *The House that Bob Built* which will give them some ideas of what will be needed.

- Ask for their help and make a plan that you can refer to as the yard is set up by them. Use the resource check list below to help.

Resources

A toy 'Bob', a toy mobile phone which 'speaks', dressing-up clothes (checked shirts and dungarees), tool sets (preferably real ones), yellow builders' hats, belt for tools, a workbench (real if possible), sets of different size screws and their containers, heavier wooden bricks, sand, wheelbarrows, wood of different lengths, pipes, shovels, measuring stick (staff), clip boards, string, pegs, plans ready drawn on large pieces of paper, red and white safety tape, water bucket, trowel, spirit levels, site safety notice with the caption: SAFETY HELMETS MUST BE WORN IN THIS AREA, a shed if outdoors or a chalked space against a wall to represent a shed.

⚠ *Safety note*

No children should be left unsupervised with heavy items or sharp tools.

- Help the class to collect and/or make what they need and then set it up – indoors or outdoors.

Teacher in role

- Play alongside the children for several days, either as one of Bob's friends, in which you facilitate the play in role, or as Bob, where you can direct the play, e.g. making a wall, as in the example below.

Directing the role-play

- Take several children outside with you and show them the plans. Have ready the tools you need – wheelbarrows, a pile of sand, shovels and bricks.

- Get the group to fill the wheelbarrows with sand, wheel it over to an empty space and tip it out.

- Then get them to roll it flat (check it with a spirit level) and then build a wall with the bricks and some of the sand. When it is done they can check that it is level.

- Take digital photographs of them at work.

- Another linked play area could be set up as a DIY store.

Resources

A space indoors for a B&Q or Homebase shop, B&Q or Homebase signs, special offer leaflets, paint colour charts, pictures of tools and any DIY captions (ask the customer services at these stores if you can have some), empty paint tins, till and credit cards scanner, receipts, shopping trolleys and a selection of items to buy.

Again, involve the children in planning and resourcing this area.

▲ *Safety note*

Make sure paint tins etc. are clean and that no children are left unsupervised with sharp or heavy tools.

Linked activities

If any parents are builders, invite them in so they can tell the children about a typical working day.

Tabby Cat's Secret by Kathy Henderson

Summary of the story

Tabby Cat's family go on holiday while their house is painted. She does not like the smell of the paint and goes off to have her kittens. When the family arrive home they have to search hard to find the kittens and bring them home.

Key events

The family go away on holiday.
Tabby Cat leaves the house because she does not like the smell of paint.
The children search everywhere for the kittens.
Their neighbour, Mr Rubenstein, finds the kittens.
The children bring the kittens home in a box.

Resources

Ask the children to bring in photographs of their own cats, a cat toy or puppet, four smaller cats (kittens), a box with a soft towel inside. Prepare some questions in advance for the teaching assistant to ask if necessary.

Drama techniques

Role-play, freeze-frame, improvisation, dynamic duos.

Early learning goals

CLL, Creative Development.

Making a start

- Ask the class to tell you any cat stories they may have.
- Show the cover and discuss what 'Tabby Cat's Secret' might be and why the girl is walking in the garden at night.
- Now read the whole story aloud.

Props

Pair/share

Teacher in role

- Show the toy cat and tell the class that when you put the cat on your lap you will become the cat – and they can ask you questions about why you went missing.

- Pair/share – now give them time to prepare the questions.

- Pick up the toy and put it on your lap and say: 'Hello, I'm the cat from the story. Would you like to ask me some questions about why I went missing?'. If children are slow to ask questions, get the teaching assistant to ask one or two questions as models for the children's own questions.

- Later, still in role as the cat, bring the box out with the towel inside it, and express surprise that the kittens are not inside. Tell the children that they must be hiding in the class somewhere and ask different children to go and find them. When they have all been found and placed safely in the box, come out of role.

Role-play: re-enacting the story

- Organise the children into pairs.

- Ask them to re-enact the scene when both children arrive home from holiday, then go searching for the cat. The dialogue in the book could be used as a script:

Children: 'Tabby Cat! Tabby Cat! Where's Tabby Cat?'
Boy: 'But look! She isn't fat any more! She's slim! She's had her kittens!'
Girl: 'Oh, Tabby Cat, show us your kittens, do!'

- Or the children could improvise their conversation, pretending to walk through the door of their home.

- The children could improvise looking everywhere – the basement, the loft, corners, cupboards, under beds, up trees, behind bushes, in the garden shed.

- They could create an area outside where they look for the kittens.

Writing activity

- Ask the children to draw a picture of a kitten hiding somewhere in the garden, then stick a flap on top that says 'Where are you?'

- Write a Big Book with the children helping you, using flaps with wording similar to those in the 'Where's Spot?' stories, e.g. Are they in the basement? No, they aren't! Are they in the loft? No, they aren't!

Dynamic duos

- Now ask them to sit opposite each other like the children in spread seven in the book (see plate section, illustration 3.2) and talk about what may happen to their kittens if they do not find them in time, as the children did in the story.

- Walk around and listen to what they are saying and ask a few to repeat their conversations with the rest of the class listening.

Freeze-frame/improvisation

- Ask the class to get into threes and decide who will be Mr Rubinstein. Ask them to freeze-frame the moment when he calls them over and shows them the kittens, then ask them to make up the conversation between Mr Rubinstein and the two children.

- Go around and listen to the conversations.

- Ask the class to get into pairs and, using mime, get them to carefully place the kittens one by one into the box and carry it home together.

Watching the whole story being enacted

- Different pairs/groups of children can be asked to act out the whole story, with the rest of the class constructively commenting on it.

Written outcomes

- The children can make little books of the story in pairs, drawing the pictures first, then adding captions. Some children may need help with this.

Making links with Knowledge and Understanding of the World

Show the children how to lay out a poster, then let them make it. This could have the title 'Looking After Kittens' with some pictures and simple captions. Use ICT software to draw a cat, or search the web using Google for kittens and cats.

'Next!', written and illustrated by Christopher Inns

Dramatic play and story sacks

This is an ideal story to be used as the basis for dramatic play. If the play area is a hospital or a doctor's surgery, direct links can be made. If not, the items which are needed can be stored in a 'story sack', along with the book. Children, with the help of a practitioner, can listen to the story and watch it come to life with the props in the sack. After a number of retellings, children can have access to the sack and act it out for themselves.

Summary of the story

Set in a toy hospital, Doctor Hopper and Nurse Rex Barker help the sick toys get better.

Key events

Doctor Hopper and Nurse Rex Barker get ready for the morning's surgery.

Rex prepares a list of patients.

Each patient files in and is treated.

Doctor and Nurse have a cup of tea.

Resources

A white coat, stethoscope and thermometer, a nurse's hat and apron, a first aid box with scissors, bandages etc., an eye chart, an assortment of toys as mentioned in the book, all with some defect, Velcro pads sewn on the toys with a special tin of missing bits which can be fixed on to repair the toys, a list of patients as shown in the book, tea set and play biscuits.

⚠ Safety note

Make sure children do not have pointed or sharp scissors.

Drama techniques

Role-play, props to support the play.

Early learning goals

The focus early learning goals for this activity are CLL and Creative Development, but a number of other goals can be supported through imaginative planning, e.g. counting in the patients and putting out five bottles of 'medicine' on a labelled shelf, looking at the toys through a magnifying glass, making 'biscuits' for the sick patients etc.

Communication, Language and Literacy

Making a start

- Show the cover of the book, read the title and ask the children where the toys are, encouraging them to think about the clues in the picture. Once this is established, encourage them to talk more about the feelings of the worried-looking doctor and nurse. Ask the children why they are worried.

Teacher in role

- Tell them you are going to be the doctor. Put on a white coat and a stethoscope and encourage the children to ask some questions by prompting them with the following words: 'Hello, I am Doctor Hopper. Thank you for asking me to your school. I have left my toy hospital for a few minutes. Would you like to ask me some questions about my hospital?' If they are not keen to ask you anything, tell them about some of the operations you have had to do, e.g. sewing on a new tail for a cat, sticking new feathers on a little bird, mending a broken arm and so on.

- Come out of role by saying 'Bye bye' and taking off your coat and stethoscope.

Reading the story

- Have the story sack ready, and as you read the story, bring out all the toys that will be in the waiting room.

- Show them the tin of bits which will be used to repair the toys.

- When you reach the page where Nurse Rex Barker holds up the list, tell the children you will need to make a list too.

- One at a time, ask different children to pick up a toy and tell you its name, then you start making the numbered list under the same heading as in the book, 'Today's Patients' (see plate section, illustration no. 3.3).

Role-play area

- If this is a doctor's surgery or a hospital, the story can be acted out with the help of a practitioner. After several pairs of children have played out the story with the practitioner, the class is likely to be able to do it independently.

Story sack

- Retell this story several times to the class and then allow children to have access to the sack. If possible, send the sack home with different children on different days to encourage parents to use it.

Writing opportunities

- Making their own lists of patients at the writing table.

- Having an appointment book where a receptionist can tick off the patients' names as they enter.

- Making labels on the computer for the medicine bottles.

- Making a list of numbers to match the items in the role-play area, e.g. three rolls of bandages, three pairs of scissors, one stethoscope, which the children can put out and tidy away every session.

- Writing and posting 'Get Well' cards to the toys, completed on the computer and printed.

- Making a Big Book called 'All About Hospitals' by sticking in their own paintings or pictures they have cut out. These can be labelled by the children.

ICT links

- Google can be used to find pictures of 'toys' and 'old toys' for discussion with the children.

Snail Trail, written and illustrated by Ruth Brown

Summary of the story

Slimy Snail sets out on his trail through the garden and finally goes to sleep.

Children will be pleasantly surprised when they realise that the huge landscape portrayed in the book is in fact a very small space in the garden – this is shown in the last double spread. They will want to read it again immediately to work it all out!

Dramatic play through story boxes and sand play

This is an ideal story to be re-enacted in a small shoebox or in a sand tray. It links two early learning goals: 'Communication, Language and Literacy' and 'Knowledge and Understanding of the World' (K&U).

Key events

Slimy Snail sets off.
He goes up a hill (a pair of garden gloves).
Through a tunnel (a flowerpot).
Into a forest (some garden canes).
Over a bridge (the handle of a basket).
Down a slope (a trowel).
Up to an arch (the prongs of a small garden fork).
Past some flowers (seed packets).
Into a cave (a garden glove).

Resources

All the items as mentioned in the book: a toy snail, garden gloves, a small garden pot with a hole in it, some sticks to represent canes, a small basket, a trowel, a garden fork, a packet of seeds; some silver foil or silver glitter to create a trail as the snail moves along; a shoebox containing sand or a large sand tray; an A3 size map of where he went with the trail stuck on in silver foil or glitter; magnifying glasses for the snail hunt.

Drama techniques

Role-play, props to support the play.

Early learning goals

The focus early learning goals for this activity are CLL, Creative Development and K&U, but a number of other goals can be supported through imaginative planning.

Making a start

- Read the book to the class.
- Read it aloud again so that the children can make sense of where the snail actually went on his travels.

Teacher in role using the props and the map

- Take the props over to the sand tray or open the shoebox containing the sand.
- Using the key events chart and the map to help you, retell the story and enlist the children's help to place the items in the correct order.
- Take the snail and ask them to tell you where he goes. As you do this, go into role as the snail, talking about what you are doing.
- Show them how to lay out the silver foil or glitter as the trail.
- Now encourage the children to play without your help. Each child could take a turn with the snail, talking through where s/he is going, in role as the snail.
- Children can create different snail trails by putting different

items into the sandbox, making tunnels, mountains, pools and so on.

Knowledge and Understanding of the World: searching for snails

- Children can go on a real snail hunt with a practitioner. Teach the children to be respectful towards these creatures and explain the importance of handling them with care, and always returning them to where they were found.

- If a real snail hunt is not possible because there is no garden area, place a number of toy snails in the outside area and go looking for them.

- Draw a map of where they were found.

ICT links

- With the children, search on Google for photos of 'snails' and 'snail trails' which the children can look at and discuss.

2.1 *Red Riding Hood*

3.1 *Bob the Builder*

The search went on for days.
"They'll grow up wild if we don't find them soon."
"What about foxes, owls and dogs?"
"Maybe we'll never find them!"
Gloom.

"Tabby Cat's wise. Trust her."

Next morning they tried to follow her
but Cat was much too sly.
She led them far away

through other people's gardens,
over walls and under fences
and always disappeared.

3.2 *Tabby Cat's Secret*

Reproduced by permission of Frances Lincoln Ltd. 4 Torriano Mews, Torriano Avenue, London NW5 2RZ

But when the leaves unfurled she came running, and cried, "Thulani, come and look! You have planted a field of sunflowers. What good are they to us? All they do is follow the sun from morning to night – just like you."

Thulani felt sad. All he wanted was to please Dora.

4.1 *The Gift of the Sun*

"Here is Osebo's drum, Nyame. And Osebo is inside."

"Well done!" said Nyame. "No-one else could get the drum. And you have taught that boastful leopard a lesson. Let him go now, and decide what you would like as your reward."

Achi-cheri looked round. All the other animals were looking jealous and cross. She thought for a moment.

"Please, Nyame," she said, "most of all I would like a hard shell to protect me from fierce animals."

4.2 *The Leopard's Drum*

When Camille and Vincent came back
from the fields, some children from
Camille's school were waiting for them.

They shouted at Vincent and threw stones.

Camille wanted them to stop – but what
could he do? He was only a small boy.
At last he ran home in tears.

5.1 *Camille and the Sunflowers*

Rama and the Demon King

An Ancient Tale from India

Jessica Souhami

5.2 Rama and the Demon King

Reproduced by permission of Frances Lincoln Ltd, 4 Torriano Mews, Torriano Avenue, London NW5 2RZ

Chapter 4

Year 1 (5–6-year-olds)

The Gift of the Sun, A Tale from South Africa by Dianne Stewart

Summary of the story

Thulani is lazy. He does not like milking the cow, so exchanges it for a goat...the goat for a sheep...the sheep for three geese...until all he has left are sunflower seeds. However, the sunflower seeds feed the hens, the hens lay more eggs – and Thulani becomes rich!

Key events

Thulani sells the cow and buys a goat.

The goat eats the corn – so Thulani buys a sheep.

Thulani sells the sheep because he does not enjoy looking after it.

He buys geese – but then sells them to buy seeds to plant.

The seeds grow into sunflowers.

He collects the seeds and feeds the hens with them.

The hens lay many eggs – so Thulani sells them and then replaces all the animals he had sold.

Thulani and his wife become rich.

Resources

Toy animals: a cow, a goat, a sheep, three geese, hens, a chick, sunflower seeds or an old sunflower seed head.

English and literacy

Speaking and listening, thinking skills.

NLS objectives Terms 2/3

5 to retell stories; 7 to discuss reasons for incidents in stories; 8 to compare and contrast stories with a variety of settings, e.g. imaginary lands and to write simple recounts.

Drama techniques

Role-play, thought tracking, dynamic duos, improvisation.

Making a start

● Show the class the cover, read out the title and ask the question 'How can the sun give a gift?'

● Direct them to pair/share and discuss this together. Hopefully, they will come up with ideas about the sun giving the gift of light, life (because plants cannot grow without it). If they do not know, discuss these with them.

Teacher in role

● Go into role as Thulani and tell them that you are feeling very happy in this picture – the sunflowers are providing lots of seeds, the hens are laying more eggs and these are hatching out into chicks – life is good – but it wasn't always that way!

● Come out of role and read the book aloud up to 'Don't you remember – the nuisance goat ate all our seed?'

Pair/share

● Ask the class to think about the reasons why Thulani and Dora are getting poorer. Ask them to pair/share their ideas.

Dynamic duo

● Divide the class into pairs – one in role as Dora, Thulani's wife, and the other as a friend of Dora's she hasn't seen for some time. Ask 'Dora' to tell her friend about what has been happening on the farm – about all the animals which Thulani has been selling, and why.

● Some can retell their conversation again, so that the class can listen. Give the class time to discuss the 'overheard conversations', e.g. what they liked and why.

Read up to the page ending with 'All he wanted was to please Dora.'

Thought tracking

● Ask the class to stand up and divide into two halves – half as Dora and half as Thulani. Go around touching them on their shoulders, asking them to think aloud their thoughts at that moment as shown in the pictures of Thulani and Dora. Encourage them to use a confident voice for Thulani and a worried voice for Dora (see plate section, illustration no. 4.1).

Writing activity

● Ask the class to write thought bubbles for both characters.

Now continue reading the book to the end.

Retelling the story

Display the list of events and get the class to practise retelling the story in small groups; then have a whole-class retelling session.

Taking it further

● Ask the class to think about the story of Jack and the Beanstalk. Ask them if there are any similarities. (Jack was lazy like Thulani, sold the cow in exchange for beans and then climbed the beanstalk.) See if they could write down the key events and improvise the story. (Some children may need to have Jack and the Beanstalk read to them as they may not know it.)

● Ask them if the setting is the same? (*The Gift of the Sun* is set in South Africa and is real, Jack and the Beanstalk is imaginary.)

Writing opportunities

- To make this easy for the children, prepare a key events list then ask the class to draw pictures for each event.

- The whole story can be structured as a recount, based on the event list.

- Demonstrate how to use the time words 'first, then, next, after that, finally' to structure the text.

- More able writers could script a scene from the book using the events list as its structure; this could be demonstrated in a guided writing session.

- A letter could be written from Dora to a friend, telling her friend about Thulani's foolish behaviour.

ICT links

Go to Google and search for pictures of South Africa and Jack and the Beanstalk. The differences between them could be discussed.

Links with other curriculum areas

Sc2 (3a,b,c); ICT (1a, 2d, 3a, 4a); Geography (3a,b,c).

Anancy and Mr Dry-Bone by Fiona French

Summary of the story

Two suitors, one rich, the other poor, attempt to win the hand of Miss Louise. Rich Mr Dry-Bone fails whereas poor, but clever, Anancy succeeds.

Key events

Mr Dry-Bone tries to make Miss Louise laugh – he changes into a cat, a pig and a rabbit, does somersaults and hangs upside down.

Miss Louise does not laugh.

Anancy borrows a jogging suit, a hunting hat, some shoes and feathers for a tie.

Miss Louise laughs at his silly clothes and they get married.

Resources

A letter from a Miss Louise, asking the class to think of ideas to make her laugh; the book, wrapped up; a second letter from Miss Louise which says she is now able to laugh, and that Fiona French, an author, has written about her in a book.

NLS objectives Year 1 Terms 1/3

5 to retell stories, giving the main points in sequence and to pick out significant incidents; 5 to describe story settings; 13 to write about significant incidents.

Drama techniques

Role-play, dynamic duos, improvisation.

Making a start

Props

- Tell the children that you have just received a very sad letter from a lady called Miss Louise who has never, ever laughed – show them the letter, and read it out. Could they suggest ways of making her laugh?

- Give the children two minutes to discuss this in pairs, and then write their suggestions up on the whiteboard (they are likely to come up with examples such as telling a joke/funny story; doing something amusing; dressing up in a funny way, etc.).

- Divide the class into small groups, and give each group one of the suggestions from the whiteboard.

- Give each group time to prepare a presentation for the rest of the class, and then ask them to perform it.

- Finish off the session by asking the class to vote on which group had the best idea – which one made them laugh the most.

Taking it further

- Get someone to bring in an urgent letter for you – and a parcel (the book wrapped up).

- Read the second letter from Miss Louise, which tells the class that she can now laugh – and that Fiona French, an author, has written her story in a book.

- Unwrap the book slowly, to build up the excitement, wondering aloud what happens to Miss Louise in the book...

- Read the whole book to them – and enjoy!

- Ask them why Anancy succeeded in making her laugh and why Mr Dry-Bone failed.

Return to the setting

- Tell the children that you are going to talk about the setting for this story – where the story takes place.

- Move through the illustrations in the book and direct their attention to key features, e.g. a very 'hot' sky, the hills, the palm trees, the tiger, the crocodile, the parrot . . . ask if they can guess where the story takes place.

ICT links

- Using Google, type in 'Caribbean', and show them real pictures of where the story took place.

Art and ICT links

- Link this story to an art lesson – and get them drawing and painting the colourful skies and hills of the Caribbean; they could use the book and downloaded pictures of the Caribbean to help them. Help the class to create frames for their pictures, through creating a repeating pattern using software or crayons to design a spider's web pattern.

Dynamic duos

- Ask them to get into twos and become people from the local town who are retelling each other the story about how Miss Louise started laughing.
- Show them the list of key events to remind them.
- Go around and listen to them – ask a few pairs to repeat their conversations with the rest of the class listening, and then ask for their views on how interesting the retelling was, and why.

Writing activity

- Ask the whole class to draw pictures of the key incidents from the story and to write matching captions.

ICT links

- Use the link below to see interesting information about spiders and Anancy: www.spyda-webb.co.uk/stories.html

Links with other curriculum areas

ICT (1a, 2d, 3a, 4a); Geography (3a,b); Art & Design (1a; 2a,b; 3a,b; 4a,b,c).

Home Before Dark, written and illustrated by Ian Beck

Summary of the story

Teddy is dropped by Lily in the park. It is a cold and windy day and he knows he must get home before dark as Lily can't go to bed without him. After several adventures he manages to get home.

Key events

Mum, Lily and Teddy go to the local park.
Teddy falls out of the pushchair and is left alone in the park.
He squeezes through the railings.
He crosses a busy road.
He is kicked about on the pavement.
He hides by the bin.
He walks up to the top of a hill and is then blown down again to his house.
He is pushed through the letterbox by the paper boy.

Resources

A teddy bear, a letter from Teddy asking children to write to Lily and tell her the real story of his adventure – the envelope has on the front the name of the class and the word URGENT.

NLS objectives Year 1 Terms 1, 2, 3

4 to predict story endings; 6 to identify and describe characters, expressing own views; 7 to prepare and retell stories through role-play in groups; 14 to write in role.

Drama techniques

Role-play, dynamic duos, freeze-frame, improvisation, decision alley.

Making a start

- Do not show the cover of the book but instead show the real teddy bear and say that this is his story.

- Read aloud the book up to the double page spread of Teddy in the park by himself.

Teacher in role

- Place Teddy on your lap and tell the children that you are now the Teddy and they can ask you about how you are feeling.

Decision alley

- Tell the children that you have to make a decision whether to leave the park or stay.

- Line up the children facing each other and as you walk down the middle in role as Teddy, one half of the class gives reasons for staying in the park, the other half gives reasons for leaving.

- Turn and tell them that you have decided to leave the park.

Writing

- Ask children to write speech bubbles telling Teddy what to do. These can be stuck around a picture of a teddy from clipart.

- Return to the book and read up to the double page spread where Teddy is walking up the hill, battling against the wind.

Role-play/thought tracking

Ask the children to individually freeze-frame Teddy walking up the hill, and go around touching them on their shoulders in order to hear his thoughts at that moment – encourage them to use a worried voice.

Taking it further

- Ask the children to come up with some ideas about what Teddy could do next.

- Pair/share – each pair to come up with some ideas which you write on a whiteboard.

- Children can choose an idea and act out the next scene using freeze-frames and improvisation.

- Read to the end of the book.

- Check the children's list of ideas to see if any of them has correctly guessed what really happened.

Dynamic duos

- Ask the pairs of children to retell the story in role, one as Teddy and one as Teddy's best friend. Give them time to discuss the 'overheard conversations', e.g. what they liked and why.

Taking it further

Letters

- The next day ask someone to deliver the letter from Teddy to your class, saying that it has the word URGENT on the envelope. The letter says that he wants the class to write to Lily telling her the true story of what happened.

Writing

● In front of the class, start writing an answer to this letter, then ask them to finish it, using the list of key events as an aid to writing if they need to.

Performance

● In groups of ten children, help them to organise a performance of the story using the key events list. Expect them to use thought tracking as the main drama technique.

ICT links

For a colour picture of the cover go to Google and type in 'Ian Beck'.

Links with other curriculum areas

ICT (1a, 2d, 3a, 4a).

The Leopard's Drum, An Asante Tale from West Africa by Jessica Souhami

Summary of the story

Osebo the leopard has a magnificent drum – and Nyame the Sky-God wants it. Nyame offers a big reward for anyone who can get it for him. Several animals try, but only one is clever enough to succeed – Achi-cheri, the tortoise!

Key events

Nyame asks Osebo if he can have his drum – but Osebo refuses.

Onini the python fails to get it.

Esono the elephant fails to get it.

Asroboa the monkey fails to get it.

Achi-cheri the tortoise tricks Osebo into getting inside the drum – and traps him!

Nyame gets the drum – frees the leopard and gives Achi-cheri a hard shell with which to protect herself.

Resources

A medium size African drum, toy leopard, snake, elephant, monkey, tortoise and a coloured photocopy of Nyame from the last but one page of the book (stuck on to card and then fixed to a stick).

NLS objectives Year 1 Term 2

4 to retell stories, giving the main points in sequence; 7 to discuss reasons for, or causes of, incidents in stories; 9 to become aware of character and dialogue, e.g. by role-playing parts; 14 to represent outlines of story plots using captions, pictures, arrows, to record main incidents in order.

Drama techniques

Role-play, dynamic duos, freeze-frame, improvisation.

Making a start

- Place all the toys except Nyame in a feely bag. Ask individual children to take turns to feel and guess which animals are in the bag.

- Then place the toys near the drum and tell the children that they are all important characters in a story.

- Ask if they can guess where the story might take place and what might happen.

- Show Nyame and ask if they can guess who he is.

- Explain who he is and that he is in the story.

- Play the drum and pass it around the group. Tell the children that this story is about Nyame wanting the drum.

Read up to 'belonged to them'

- Give the children time to scan the pictures, noting that the toys which were in the feely bag all appear in this story.

- Read the first line, emphasising the words 'fierce', 'proud' and 'boastful'.

- Read the second line then beat out a rhythm on the drum to add some drama.

- Continue reading, then place each toy character near the drum.

Read up to 'And Nyame disappeared'

- Read the next two pages, emphasising the words 'wonderful', 'I', 'lend' and 'try'.

- Ask how the pictures tell us that Nyame is the Sky-God.

- Ask the children what challenge Nyame has given, and why any of the animals might accept the challenge.

Teacher in role

- Tell the class that when you pick up the stick puppet of Nyame, you will be Nyame and they can ask you some questions about what has happened so far.

- Give them a little pair/share time to prepare some questions.

- Go into role and answer any questions they ask.

Look at the 3rd spread.

- Out of role let the class spend some time enjoying this picture, then read the text aloud.

- Ask them to guess if he will succeed.

- Read the text on the 4th spread, making sure that you say 'Looking for me, Onini?' in a really nasty, sinister voice.

Read up to 'Just looking…fine…huge…mag…ni…fi…cen…t…'

Children in role

- Divide the class into threes. Each trio will be the snake, the elephant and the monkey. Ask them to tell you why they did not take the drum from the leopard.

Read the 9th spread.

- Now tell the class that Achi-Cheri does succeed in taking the drum to Nyame.

- Ask them to pair/share and try to guess how she does it.

- Write up their guesses in a list large enough for them to see.

Now read to the end of the book.

- Refer to the children's list of ideas. Discuss whether anyone had guessed correctly.

- Ask why Achi-Cheri chose the shell above anything else she might have chosen.

Teacher in role

Go into role as Nyame, retelling the story and adding your own thoughts about what has happened (see plate section, illustration no. 4.2).

Retelling the story

- Start beating the drum while the children make a circle.

- Ask the children to form pairs and, in turn, to collect one toy character and 'Nyame', the stick puppet.

- Encourage the children to improvise the retelling of different parts of the story while sitting beside the drum.

Freeze-frame/improvisation

Now get the class to produce a series of freeze-frames and improvisations for the whole story; choose a selection of the children to perform this as a play and get the class to comment on their performance.

Writing

- Ask the children to form pairs and draw pictures to match the key events list (storyboard the story) and then add their own captions.

ICT/Art links

- ICT – use Google to search for pictures of 'leopards' and 'Nyame'. The latter has a link to the Oxfam website where there is some interesting information on Ashanti fabric designs. It also shows the symbol for God and its meaning – see below.

- Help the class to make potato prints based on designs from this website, and produce some brightly coloured cloth as in the end pages of the book.

9. GYE NYAME.
Lit. Only God.
Symbolizes the greatness
and power of God. Only
God can see where we've
gone and where we're
going.

Links with other curriculum areas

Sc2 (3a,b,c); ICT (1a, 2d, 3a, 4a); Geography (3a,b); Art and Design (1a; 2a,b; 3a,b; 4a,b,c).

Chapter 5

Year 2 (6–7-year-olds)

Camille and the Sunflowers, A Story about Vincent Van Gogh, written and illustrated by Laurence Anholt

Summary of the story

The Big Book version is a delight, celebrating the power of the artist through Anholt's powerful illustrations (see plate section, illustration no. 5.1). It offers a glimpse of the painter's life through the eyes of a young boy, Camille, and develops an awareness of the importance of friendship which can combat, but not always overcome, local prejudice towards a stranger in town.

Key events

Vincent arrives in Camille's town.

Camille's father and Camille help him settle in.

Vincent paints Camille's whole family.

Children in the town show their dislike of Vincent.

Camille delivers a letter to Vincent from the townspeople asking him to leave.

Vincent leaves the town.

Resources

Postcards of a selection of Van Gogh's works, including those featured in the book; a bunch of real or artificial sunflowers; website information about Van Gogh; a set of cards with the following captions: Who?, What?, When?, Where?, Why?, How?; a digital camera.

NLS objectives

4 to predict story endings; 6 to identify and describe characters, expressing own views; 7–14 to write in role.

Drama techniques

Role-play, dynamic duos, freeze-frame, improvisation, decision alley, performance of the key events in the book.

Making a start

- Display the cover and give pupils time to 'search-read' the illustration.

- Give out the question/caption cards or display these where they can be seen. Ask the class to pair/share their ideas about what's happening in the picture, and then each think of a question beginning with one of the caption cards.

- Ask them to tell you the question, then you ask the class for possible answers, so that the views of the whole class are shared.

- Read up to the end of the 4th spread: 'Vincent was very pleased to have two good friends'.

Teacher in role

- Say that you are about to go into role as Camille's father, then Camille (about 2 mins each).

- Ask the children to think of some questions.

- Go into role, saying that you have only a few minutes to spare as you have to get back to work (as Camille's father) or play (as Camille).

- Come out of role and ask them to pair/share what might happen on the following pages.

- List their ideas on a sheet of paper or on a smart board to return to it the next day.

Taking it further

- Ask pupils to sit in a circle.

- Read up to the end of the 9th spread: . . . 'learn to love Vincent's paintings'.

Dynamic duos

- Ask the children to turn to face each other in pairs 'in role' as two children being spiteful about Vincent, and saying horrible things about him.

- Walk around the outside of the group listening to their talk.

- Use a signal for them to stop – and ask three or four pairs of dynamic duos to carry on their conversations, with the rest of the class listening.

- Now ask the pairs to go into role as Camille and his father. Ask them what Camille's father might be saying to Camille in the picture on the last page they have read.

- Read up to the last spread: 'and ran out of the yellow house into the sunshine'.

Decision alley

- Divide the class into two halves. Ask each half to discuss in pairs reasons why Vincent should have gone or stayed.

- Now ask them to line up facing each other. Walk down the middle in role as Vincent, listening to what they are saying.

- At the end turn around and tell them what you have decided.

- Ask the class to divide into small groups to retell the story. Then ask each group to present it to the class.

Children planning the play

- Display the key events list and help the class to plan a series of freeze-frames and improvisations. Give the children time to discuss and comment on the performance of the different groups.

- Use a digital camera to record each scene and then ask pupils to print these scenes and display them on a wall with captions, preferably in a corridor display.

Writing opportunities

The experience of planning and performing the play will lead to a rich variety of writing opportunities, e.g.:

- Retelling the story in their own words, using the key events chart.

- Writing a letter to a friend 'in role' as Camille or Vincent. The letters can be stuck into a Big Book which can be decorated with the children's own art.

- Giving time for different groups to research information about Van Gogh and produce a small A4 folded book on Van Gogh. Each page could have headings, for instance 'Where He Painted'; 'What He Painted'. The front could be a cover picture of Sunflowers (using software), and a blurb could be written for the back cover.

- Children can use Google in order to create a folder of pictures; if they use the following link they can see the portraits which are in the book: www.aidmilne-plus.com/downloadsportraits.htm.

Links with other curriculum areas

Sc2 (3a,b,c); ICT (1a, 2d, 3a, 4a); History (6c); Geography (3a,b); Art and Design (1a; 2a,b; 3a,b; 4a,b,c); PSHE and Citizenship (1a,b; 2a,c; 4e).

Rama and the Demon King, An Ancient Tale from India, retold and illustrated by Jessica Souhami

Summary of the story

This is the story of the brave and good prince Rama and his battle against Ravana, the evil ten-headed king of all demons. When Rama is wrongfully banished to the forest, Ravana uses a fiendish trick to kidnap the prince's beautiful wife, Sita. Rama enlists the help of an army of fearless monkeys and their amazing leader Hanuman to rescue Sita and regain his kingdom (see plate section, illustration no. 5.2).

Key events

The king sends Rama away to the forest, but Sita and Laksman go with him.

Rama and Lakshman kill thousands of demons.

Ravana is angry and decides to kidnap Sita.

Rama and Hanuman rescue Sita by building an amazing bridge.

Ravana is killed by Rama in a terrible battle.

Rama and Sita return to India and are made king and queen.

Resources

Four caption cards from the 4th spread (see below); some Indian music; percussion; sound effects.

NLS objectives Year 2 Term 2

4 to predict story endings; 6 to identify and describe characters, expressing own views; 7 to prepare and retell stories through role-play in groups; 14 to write in role.

Drama techniques

Role-play, dynamic duos, freeze-frame, improvisation, decision alley, class meeting.

Making a start

- Display the cover and give pupils time to 'search-read' the illustration.

- Tell them this is Ravana, the ten-headed king of all the demons.

- Explain that demons are very bad – they do wicked things.

- Reveal the captions you have written up from the 4th spread:

    > No one can defeat me.
    > No one is stronger than me.
    > No one is more cunning.
    > No one knows so much magic.

- Get the whole class to practise saying this loudly, in readiness for when Ravana makes his first appearance in the book.

Read up to the end of the 2nd spread: '. . . to face the dangers of the forest together'.

Teacher in role

- Tell the class you are about to go into role as the king – ask them to pair/share and think of some questions to ask him.

- Now go into role as the king and answer their questions.

- Ask the pupils to pair/share again and predict what dangers Sita, Lakshman and Rama might face.

Decision alley

- Divide the class into two halves facing each other; ask a boy and a girl to role-play Sita and Lakshman and walk down the middle of the alley.

- Ask one side to give reasons why they should go with Rama, the other why they should stay.

- At the end ask them to say that they will go with Rama.

- Read up to the end of the 4th spread: 'And he quivered with rage'.

- Encourage the class to boast again when the captions appear in the text!

Read up to the end of the 10th spread: '. . . is full of monsters'.

Teacher in role/meeting

- Divide the class into groups of four and ask them to come up with ways of rescuing Sita.

- Ask one pupil in each group to write down the group's ideas on to paper.

- Spend ten minutes on this and then go into role as Rama and call the children together for a meeting where they can put forward their ideas to you, in role. Accept each idea in turn from the groups, commenting on the strengths and possible weaknesses of their rescue plans.

- This could be the basis for the next lesson, where each group acts out what they do to rescue Sita, rehearsing their rescue attempts and improvising dialogue as they act it out.

- Ask the class to comment on the performance of each group.

Read up to the end of the 20th spread: 'Ravana was DEAD'.

Dynamic duos

- Ask the class to divide into pairs then to role-play two monkeys who had been part of the rescue plan and ensuing battle.

- Ask them to retell this part of the story to each other. As they do this, walk around the class and listen to them.

- After two minutes, stop them and select several pairs to carry on their conversations in front of the rest of the class.

Read the last spread.

- Using the key events chart, ask the class to practise retelling the story to each other.

Children planning the play

- Display the key events list, and help the class to plan a series of freeze-frames and improvisations. Give children time to discuss and comment on the performance of the different groups.

- Indian music could be played as an introduction to the play, and cymbals clashed when Ravana appears.
- Use a digital camera to record each scene and then ask children to print these scenes and display them on a wall with captions, preferably in a corridor display.

Writing opportunities

The experience of planning and performing the play will lead to a rich variety of writing opportunities, e.g.

- Spread 2: The king writing a sad letter to a friend telling him what the stepmother has made him do.
- Spread 10: Labelling drawings of plans on how to rescue Sita.
- Spread 20: Writing dialogue. These could be based on the dynamic duos or the children could draw a picture of two monkey heads and write some of the conversation in speech bubbles.
- Last spread: A wedding invitation decorated with Indian art.

ICT links

Type in 'Rama' on Google and download pictures which children can see and discuss together.

Links with other curriculum areas

Sc2 (3a,b,c); ICT (1a, 2d, 3a, 4a); History (6c); Geography (3a,b); Art and Design (1a; 2a,b; 3a,b; 4a,b,c); PSHE and Citizenship (1a,b; 2a,c; 4e).

Little Inchkin by Fiona French

Summary of the story

This is a charming story of a Japanese 'Tom Thumb', whose determination to prove himself results in a glittering prize – normal stature and the hand of a beautiful princess.

Key events

Hana and Tanjo visit the temple and ask for a child.

Inchkin is born but his parents do not love him.

He leaves home to seek his fortune.

He becomes a skilled swordsman.

Prince Sanjo asks Inchkin to protect his daughter on a journey to a temple.

He fights off two demons and saves her life.

Inchkin grows tall and marries the princess.

Resources

A paper lotus flower and a tiny doll; a ruler with measurements in inches; copies of the Tom Thumb story; a small collection of Japanese artefacts to assist in looking at the art work, e.g. dish, teacup, vase; Japanese music, cymbals, bells.

Drama techniques

Role-play, freeze-frame, thought tracking.

NLS objectives Year 2 Terms 2/3

2 to investigate the style and voice of traditional story language;
3 to identify typical story themes, e.g. weak over strong; 3 to

identify and discuss main characters; 7 to describe and sequence key incidents in a variety of ways; 10 to write sustained stories.

Making a start

Show the cover and ask the class where the story is set – and how they know.

Read the first double page spread, beginning 'Long ago in old Japan . . .'.

- Give pupils time to look at the illustrations and explain that the big statue on the left is the Buddha, which is inside the temple.
- Ask a few children to ring some percussion bells gently as you turn to the cover once more.
- Read the text aloud, whispering when Hana speaks and speaking in an authoritative way when Buddha speaks.
- Ask them if it sounds like a fairy story – if they agree, ask why ('Long ago in old Japan . . .').

Teacher in role

- Read the 2nd spread text in a scornful voice as Hana speaks.
- Ask the children why the parents had named him Inchkin. Show them a ruler with inches marked on it.

- Tell the class to pair/share and think of some questions to ask Hana about why she does not love her child.
- Go into role as Hana, holding the paper lotus flower and the doll inside it, and ask the class to ask you some questions.

Out of role, read the 3rd and 4th spreads.

- Ask the class what they know now about Inchkin from reading these two spreads.

Writing activity

- Ask the class to talk about, then write down what they know about Hana and about Inchkin.

Children in role

Read the 5th and 6th spreads.

- Ask the class to pair/share and discuss why Prince Sanjo chose Inchkin to protect his daughter.

- Tell them to all go into role as Prince Sanjo and ask them questions, e.g. 'Why did you choose such a little warrior?'; 'How can Inchkin possibly save your daughter from wicked demons or dragons which might appear?'; 'What will you do if he runs away?'; 'What will you do if he stays and fights off evil demons?'

Read the 7th to 10th spreads.

- Ask the pupils what will happen next. If they come up with the idea of a reward of some kind, ask if they can guess what Inchkin's dearest wish might be.

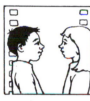

Freeze-frame/thought tracking

- Read the text on the 11th spread and ask the class to form freeze-frames in pairs – Inchkin and the princess. Go around each pair, tapping them on the shoulder and asking them to think aloud their thoughts.

Read the 12th spread.

- Ask whether the story sounds like a typical fairy tale.

- Go on to ask them what the theme of the book is (weak over strong).

Children planning the play

- Display the key events list and help the class to plan a series of freeze-frames and improvisations. Give children time to discuss and comment on the performance of the different groups.

- Use a digital camera to record each scene and then ask pupils to print these scenes and display them on a wall with captions – preferably in a corridor display.

- Ask them to organise the music to accompany the play.

- Read Tom Thumb to the class, and ask the class to compare the two stories and say what is the same and what is different and then retell the story in their own words.

- Ask the children what these two stories are really about (the power of being brave even though it may seem impossible to overcome the difficulties, e.g. small stature).

Writing opportunities

- Give the class time to plan, draft, edit and publish their own stories based on *Little Inchkin*. Suggest that they decorate the covers of their books using ideas from the artefacts or from the designs found in *Little Inchkin*.

ICT links

Search Google for Tom Thumb books in order to see the covers. Suggest the children design a book cover for their own story.

Cross-curricular

Make links with PSHE and Citizenship, Art and Design.

The Fire Children, A West African Folk Tale, retold by Eric Maddern

Summary

Two spirit people are sneezed out of the mouth of Nyame, the Sky-God. They land on Earth and make their home in a cave. Aso Yaa is lonely and decides to make some secret clay children to keep her company. Nyame keeps making surprise visits so that they are never properly baked and are all different colours. When it is safe to do so, Aso Yaa and her friend, Kwaku Ananse, make them come to life. When the fire children grow up they go to live all over the world, which is why the people in the world are all different colours.

Key events

Nyame makes the planet Earth and then a round trapdoor in the sky so that he can visit it.

He looks through the trapdoor and sneezes – and two spirit people land on Earth.

The man, Kwaku Ananse, and the woman, Aso Yaa, decide to live in a cave.

Aso Yaa makes some clay children because she is lonely.

Nyame keeps visiting, so the man and woman have to keep taking the clay children out of the fire.

The clay figures are brought to life – and are all different colours.

The children grow up and go to live all around the world.

Resources

Stick puppets (photocopy on to card Nyame's head from the 8th spread and the spirit people from the 9th spread and fix each one on to a stick); African music; drums and cymbals.

NLS objectives

4 to predict story endings; 5 to discuss story settings; 6 to identify and describe characters; 7 to prepare and retell stories individually; 13 to use story settings from own readings; 14 to write character profiles.

Drama techniques

Role-play, dynamic duos, freeze-frame, improvisation, decision alley.

Making a start

- Show the end pages and ask them to guess where the story is set (West Africa) and to say why.

Read up to the end of the 4th spread: '. . . and dance with the falling leaves'.

Role-play

- Hold up the stick puppets of Kwaku Ananse and Aso Yaa.
- Tell the class to prepare some questions to ask the two spirit people, who will come to life when you hold them up again.

Read up to the end of the 7th spread: '. . . and then he disappeared'.

Children and teacher in role

- Hold up the two stick puppets again and tell the children to go into role as the spirit people and to answer Nyame when he speaks.

- Bring out the third stick puppet and in a booming voice repeat what Nyame says in the book. The class should reply as on the last page of the 7th spread.

Based on what they have listened to so far in the story, ask pairs of children to make a character chart like the one below, and then start filling it in. Suggest that under each name they write what sort of a person that character is.

Nyame	Aso Yaa	Kwaku Ananse

Read to the end of the book.

Dynamic duos

- Ask the children to go into role as a fire person who is telling the story of their beginnings to a child.

Children planning the play

- Display the key events list, and help the class to plan a series of freeze-frames and improvisations. Give the children time to discuss and comment on the performance of the different groups.

- African music could be played as an intro to the play, and cymbals clashed when Nyame appears.

- Use a digital camera to record each scene and then ask pupils to print these scenes and display them on a wall with captions, preferably in a corridor display.

Writing opportunities

Ask the class to complete their character charts in pairs, then write a description of one or more of the characters, supported by a picture they have drawn themselves.

ICT links

Use Google to search for 'Nyame' and pictures of West Africa.

Links with other curriculum areas

Sc2 (3a,b,c); ICT (1a, 2d, 3a, 4a); History (6c); Geography (3a,b); Art and Design (1a; 2a,b; 3a,b; 4a,b,c); PSHE and Citizenship (1a,b; 2a,c; 4e).

Appendix 1

Monitoring the impact of the use of drama linked to books and across the curriculum: Foundation Stage and Key Stage 1

Foundation Stage

Children	Teacher
Creative development	***Planning***
● 2 use props to support role-play	● Plans for coverage of the objectives on a weekly basis
● 3 Role-play characters in his/her play	
● 7 Act out a story	● Plans that the children take part in setting up the role-play areas
● 8 Sustain role-play	
● 9 Make comments on the drama work e.g. likes/dislikes	● Plans indoor and outdoor role-play
	● Facilitates 'small-world play' dramatic scenarios
Language for communication and thinking	
	Speaking/Listening/Drama
● 2 Talk and listen during role-play	● Plans for herself and practitioners to regularly play alongside the children 'in role' as a means of fostering engagement and modelling talk
● 3 Act out a role	
● 5 Recreate roles and experiences	
● 6 Interact with others	● Assesses for quality of speaking, listening, thinking and engagement in the activities
● 7 Use talk to clarify thinking, feelings and events	
● 8 Speak clearly, showing awareness of the listener	● Observes children in role independently
● 9 Give relevant detail e.g. vocabulary	● Encourages children to reflect on the quality of the role-play
Reading	***Reading***
● 1 Are developing interest in books	● 'Teacher in role' used as the main way to get children to think, discuss, reflect and respond to the characters in the story and their situation
● 5 Show an understanding of the elements of stories	
● 7 Retell narratives in the correct sequences	
Writing	***Writing***
● 6 Attempt writing for a variety of purposes	● Children write 'in role' for a real purpose as a response to the book

Early Years Co-ordinator	Head Teacher
Subject leadership Advises teachers on: • how to use drama techniques to support learning objectives • which resources to use • how to plan a brief but effective weekly plan which supports speaking and listening, creativity, reading and writing **Assesses for a consistent approach** • Monitors teaching to ensure all of the above is in place • Helps teachers to assess the impact on speaking, listening, thinking, reading and writing **Supports staff** • Coaches staff on how to run sessions • Organises staff meetings to train staff and share best practice within the school	**Leadership** • Has a clear commitment to drama • Understands the pedagogy with the links to accelerated learning and engagement of all pupils • Sees drama as an entitlement in the creative delivery of the curriculum **Assesses for consistency across the school** • Expects that all children in every class will have access to drama as a key learning tool • Tracks the impact on learning across the school using an 'attitude and progress' analysis grid linked to speaking, listening, thinking, reading and writing **Support** • Ensures key staff are trained in using drama techniques • Plans joint visits with Early Years Co-ordinator to monitor teaching and learning and assess impact

Key Stage 1 (Year 1 and Year 2)

Children	Teacher
'Speaking, Listening, Learning: *Progression in Drama*' Through discussion or from shared reading of a book, they should be able to: ● develop work in role ● create characters imaginatively ● talk about different characters' actions and feelings ● say what they enjoyed or liked about what they have seen or heard ***NLS Reading Objectives:*** **Y1/Y2T2** ● 4 retell stories, giving the main points in sequence ● 7 discuss reasons for, or causes of, incidents in stories ● 8 identify and discuss characters ● 9 become aware of character and dialogue by role-playing parts ● 4 predict story endings ***NLS Writing Objectives:*** ● 15 build simple profiles of characters ● 16 use some of the elements of known stories to structure own writing ● 10 write sustained stories	***Planning*** ● Plans for coverage of the objectives on a weekly basis ***Speaking/Listening/Drama*** ● Plans for herself to play regularly alongside the children 'in role' as a means of fostering engagement and modelling talk ● Assesses for quality of speaking, listening, thinking and engagement in the activities ● Observes children in role independently ● Encourages children to reflect on the quality of the role-play ***Reading*** ● Uses a range of drama techniques to give children the skills to retell stories ● Ensures children identify closely with characters through discussion and role-play ● Asks children to predict endings ● Plans for class to act out key moments in the story, improvising dialogue based on the text ***Writing*** ● Ensures they write 'in role' as characters ● Asks for sustained stories

Literacy Co-ordinator	Head Teacher
Subject leadership	**Leadership**
Advises teachers on:	• Has a clear commitment to drama
• how to use drama techniques to support learning objectives	• Understands the pedagogy with the links to accelerated learning and engagement of all pupils
• which resources to use	• Sees drama as an entitlement in the creative delivery of the curriculum
• how to plan a brief but effective weekly plan which supports speaking and listening, creativity, reading and writing	**Assesses for consistency across the school**
Assesses for a consistent approach	• Expects that all children in every class will have access to drama as a key learning tool
• Monitors teaching to ensure all of the above is in place	• Tracks the impact on learning across the school using an 'attitude and progress' analysis grid linked to speaking, listening, thinking, reading and writing
• Helps teachers to assess the impact on speaking, listening, thinking, reading and writing	
Supports staff	**Support**
• Coaches staff on how to run sessions	• Ensures key staff are trained in using drama techniques
• Organises staff meetings to train staff and share best practice within the school	• Plans joint visits with literacy co-ordinators to monitor teaching and learning and assess impact

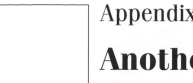

Appendix 2

Another 15 useful books for drama

Foundation Year

Rosie's Walk by Pat Hutchins, published by Puffin
ISBN: 0 14 050032 4

We're Going on a Bear Hunt by Helen Oxenbury, published by
Walker Books ISBN: 0 7445 2323 0

Owl Babies by Martin Waddell, published by Walker Books
ISBN: 0 7445 3167 5

Copy Me, Copycub by Richard Edwards, published by Frances
Lincoln ISBN: 0 7112 1420 4

I Want My Dummy! by Tony Ross, published by Collins
ISBN: 0 00 712298 5

Year 1

Ponko and the South Pole by Meredith Hooper, published by
Frances Lincoln ISBN: 0 7112 1942 7

The Gruffalo by Julia Donaldson, published by Macmillan
ISBN: 0 333 71093 2

Mr Wolf's Pancakes by Jan Fearnley, published by Mammoth
ISBN: 0 7497 3559 7

Mine! by Hiawyn Oram, published by Frances Lincoln
ISBN: 0 7112 0682 1

The Monster Bed by Jeanne Willis, published by Red Fox
ISBN: 0 09 955320 1

Year 2

Grace and Family by Mary Hoffman, published by Frances Lincoln ISBN: 0 7112 0869 7

A Lovely Bunch of Coconuts by Dennis Reader, published by Walker Books ISBN: 0 7445 1763 X

Dear Daddy by Philippe Dupasquier, published by Puffin ISBN: 0 14 050540 7

Stories from the Ballet by Margaret Greaves, published by Frances Lincoln ISBN: 0 7112 2162 6

The Hodgeheg by Dick King-Smith, published by Puffin ISBN: 0 14 032503 4

In addition to these, of course, there are many collections of traditional tales!